SHANGHAI

上海市人民政府新闻办公室编
上海辞书出版社出版

COMPILED BY INFORMATION OFFICE OF SHANGHAI MUNICIPALITY
PUBLISHED BY SHANGHAI LEXICOGRAPHIC PUBLISHING HOUSE

上海市市标

The emblem of Shanghai

前　言

　　上海——这座太平洋西海岸重要的港口城市,正以其神话般的故事引来世界的注目。

　　岁月悠悠,沧海桑田。上海,这个闻名于世的大都市曾是诞生于黄浦江畔的一个小渔村。历史上的上海,曾凭藉位居中国黄金海岸与黄金水道交汇点这一得天独厚的区位优势,逐步发展成为远东地区著名的金融贸易中心和近代文明的大都市。历史上称其为"江海通津,东南都会"。勤劳的上海人民曾挥洒时间的巨笔,饱蘸黄浦江水写下上海历史灿烂的一页。

　　然而,更为辉煌的记录还是在今天。当人类进入20世纪90年代,历史再一次垂青于这座城市,改革开放使上海呈现出一片生机勃勃的景象:新建的南浦、杨浦、奉浦、徐浦大桥横跨浦江之上,气势雄伟,蔚为壮观;三条江底隧道宛如火龙穿穴,把浦东浦西紧紧相联;亚洲第一高度的东方明珠广播电视塔,巍峨屹立,光彩夺目;市内郊外一座座高楼大厦拔地而起,一片片市民新居草木葱茏,一条条高架道路越城而过;海内外有识之士纷纷看好上海,中外合作之花盛开浦江两岸;体现群众文化色彩的广场音乐会,不断奏响上海在前进的动人乐曲。在邓小平理论指引下,上海已经站在中国改革开放的前沿,正在发生着划时代的巨变。今日的上海已进入一个崭新的历史阶段。

　　上海是一个充满活力的城市,优越的地理条件,深沉的文化积淀,坚实的经济基础,悠久的中外经济、文化交流历史,形成了这个城市取之不尽的独特资源,也使上海充满勃勃生机。人类社会即将跨入21世纪,在迈向新世纪的伟大进程中,上海人民正坚定不移地实施尽快把上海建设成为国际经济、金融、贸易中心之一的发展战略,上海人在创造着更美好的明天,上海这个城市永远年轻。

FOREWORD

Shanghai, a major port city on the west coast of the Pacific, is undergoing the most spectacular growth during its 150 — year history as an open port. Its success story is attracting the attention of the world.

Located where the Yangtze River, China's largest river, joins the country's prosperous eastern coast, Shanghai has evolved from a small 19th century fishing town into a modern metropolis and a renowned financial and trade centre in East Asia. The city is the country's largest port with a transportation network extending to China's vast inland regions.

In recent years, Shanghai has scored great achievements in its endeavor to become one of the world's economic, financial and trade centres. The city was pushed to the forefront of China's reform and opening in 1990 and was offered a rare historical opportunity to carry out its development. After years of reform and opening, Shanghai has taken on a new look of prosperity.

The city has carried out massive urban reconstruction, and its appearance keeps changing. The new Nanpu, Yangpu and Xupu bridges now span over the Huangpu River. Along with the Oriental Pearl TV Tower in Pudong, they have formed a modern landscape in Shanghai. The three Huangpu River tunnels link Pudong with Puxi (West Shanghai). The elevated highways, mushrooming high — rises and new residential areas have greatly improved the city's investment environment and lured a growing number of multinationals to launch projects in Shanghai. The city has entered a new period of rapid development.

Shanghai is full of vitality. Its favorable geographic location, rich cultural heritage, solid economic foundation and a long history of East — West exchanges have all contributed to the city's spectacular growth. As the 21st Century approaches, the people of Shanghai will embrace both opportunities and challenges, and work hard to turn their city into one of the world's major business centres. The city of Shanghai is forever young.

CONTENTS 目录

● 城 市 新 貌
● 历 史 名 城
● 人 民 生 活
● 经 济 建 设
● 社 会 发 展
● 对 外 交 往

● A NEW LOOK
● A RICH HISTORY
● THE PEOPLE
● ECONOMIC PROGRESS
● SOCIAL LIFE
● OPENING TO THE OUTSIDE WORLD

城市新貌

A NEW LOOK

上海是繁华的城市,发展中的城市,富有朝气的城市。

上海港是东方大港,世界第三。它与世界上160多个国家和地区的400多个港口有运输往来,港口吞吐量雄居世界前茅。上海港沿黄浦江绵延深入,两岸高楼耸立,码头缀连,吊车参天,巨轮鸣笛,气势磅礴。上海虹桥国际空港,银鹰翱翔,遨游中华,飞向世界。上海铁路、公路如织,通向四面八方。

有人说,上海长高了。上海曾被誉为"世界建筑博览会":有仿古典、欧洲皇宫、西班牙、挪威等式花园别墅;也有"从苏伊士运河到远东白令海峡最华贵的办公大楼"。但是,当年被称为"远东第一高楼"的国际饭店,也不过是24层。到1997年底,上海超过20层的高楼已有966幢。当年的国际饭店也只能算是小弟弟了。

上海的马路呈棋盘形,大多以全国的省、市、县名命名。随着城市的发展,上海以全新的面貌展现在世人面前。新建成的内环高架路,环绕上海市区,联结浦东浦西,复道行空,绵延47.66公里。在市中心,贯通东西、南北的高架路已突兀而起。从上海火车站至梅陇的地铁一号线已延伸到莘庄。从虹桥机场至浦东国际机场的地铁二号线也正在建设中。形成了从地面到高空、从地上到地下立体的现代化交通网络。

Shanghai is a prosperous and dynamic city. Shanghai Port is the country's largest and ranks third in the world. It is linked with more than 400 ports in about 160 countries and regions. The Hongqiao International Airport can handle more than 10 million passengers a year. The city is also linked with other Chinese cities by railways and highways.

Known as the "Museum of World Architecture", Shanghai has houses and buildings of classical Chinese, European, Japanese and modern styles. The city has grown taller. The Park Hotel, which was once the highest building in the Far East, is now dwarfed by many new skyscrapers. The city had counted 966 high-rise buildings with 20 stories and more by the end of 1997.

The streets of Shanghai are named after Chinese provinces, cities and counties. The elevated Inner Ring Road, 47.66 kilometres long, surrounds the city proper and links Pudong with Puxi. Another elevated highway runs from south to north through the city's downtown area. The subway Metro Line One runs from the Shanghai Railway Station to Xinzhuang. A multi — tiered traffic network has emerged in Shanghai.

Nanjing Road, Huaihai Road and Sichuan Road are symbols of Shanghai's prosperity. When night falls, these shopping streets glitter with neon lights, transforming the city into a modern wonderland.

The Bund along the Huangpu River was once known as the "Wall Street of Far East" with 44 banks.

Today, it has been restored as the financial centre of the city.

Shanghai is expanding. The Hongqiao Development Area, the Caohejin High — Tech Park, the Minhang Economic Development Zone and the Pudong New Area have given impetus to the city's development. A number of satellite towns have also formed around Shanghai, such as the petrochemical town of Jinshan, the steel — making town of Baoshan and the automobile town of Huating.

设施一流,馆藏极丰的上海博物馆新馆1996年10月在人民广场建成开馆
Located in People's Square, the new building of Shanghai Museum was inaugurated in October 1996. It boasts world-class facilities and a vast collection of cultural relics and art works.

上海图书馆新馆1996年12月开馆
The new building of Shanghai Library stands around the corner of Huaihai
Road M. and Gao'an Road. It was opened to the public in December 1996.

上海大剧院的建筑设计和设备配置达到了世界一流水平
Shanghai Grand Theatre has world-class
architectural designs and facilities.

上海体育场可容纳8万名观众
The new Shanghai Stadium can
seat 80,000 spectators.

耗资数亿元建造的中心绿地使陆家嘴金融
贸易区的环境更为优美
The Central Park has greatly improved the
environment of the Lujiazui Finance and Trade
Zone. Its construction has costed hundreds of
millions of yuan.

浦东陆家嘴金融贸易区的形态开发和功能
开发俱获进展

The booming Lujiazui business district in
Pudong.

外滩对岸的浦东滨江大道别有一番风光

The beautiful Riverside Avenue faces the Bund
across the Huangpu River.

东方明珠广播电视塔是今日上海
的标志性新景观之一

The Oriental Pearl TV Tower has
become a new landmark of Shanghai.

1991年11月建成通车的南浦大桥是上海市区第一座跨越黄浦江的大桥
The Nanpu Bridge, opened to traffic in November 1991, is the first bridge over the Huangpu River in urban Shanghai.

1993年10月建成通车的杨浦大桥，其主跨径居当时世界同类桥梁之首
Built in October 1993, the Yangpu Bridge has the world's longest central span for this type of cable－stayed suspension bridge.

延安东路隧道先后建成北线和南线的两个独立通道
The Yan'an Road Tunnel has two one－way tubes for auto traffic.

黄浦江是上海的母亲河，也是上海境内最大的水上通道
The Huangpu River is the mother river of Shanghai
and the largest waterway running through the city.

1997年6月建成通车的徐浦大桥是上海外
环线的组成部分
Constructed in June 1997 the Xupu Bridge
is part of the city's Qutter Ring Road.

虹桥国际机场的年旅客吞吐量与上海市总人口相近

The Hongqiao International Airport has an annual passenger volume almost equal to the entire population of Shanghai.

地铁一号线设有16个站点
The subway Metro Line One has 16 stations.

漕溪路立交桥是上海内环高架路和沪闵高架路的交点

The Caoxi Road Overpass is the crossing point of the Inner Ring Road and the Humin Highway.

上海广场　　Shanghai Plaza

梧桐、油画、庭院灯构成了衡山路的优雅景观
Plane trees, oil paintings and lampposts compose a romantic scenery along Hengshan Road.

孩子们爱与广场鸽为伴
Children play with pigeons in People's Square.

众多公园发挥着平衡市区生态环境的功能
Numerous parks help improve the local
ecological system.

通过改造铁路上海站周围旧区发展起来的
不夜城商业中心

The Kerry Everbright City is an upstart
commercial centre near the Shanghai Railway
Station.

成熟的投资环境使虹桥经济技术开发区单
位面积吸收的外资数额在各开发区中位居
前茅

The Hongqiao Development Area leads other
economic zones in Shanghai in absorbing
foreign investment, measured by per square
metre.

林荫大道
A tree－covered boulevard
in western Shanghai.

位于松江县天马山上的护珠塔建于1079年，
塔身倾斜30°而不倒

Huzhu Pagoda in Songjiang County was
erected in 1079 and is leaning 30 degrees off
the plumb.

位于松江县的西林塔建于1265—1274年间，
是上海现存最高的古塔

The Xilin Pagoda in Songjiang County, built
between 1265 – 1274, is the tallest surviving
pagoda in Shanghai.

位于金山区松隐镇的华严塔建于1380年

Huayan Pagoda in Songying Town, Jinshan
District, dates back to 1380.

位于嘉定区的法华塔建于1205—1207年间

Fahua Pagoda in Jiading District was
constructed between 1205 – 1207.

位于松江县的兴圣教寺塔(松江方塔)建于1068年

Square Pagoda in Songjiang County has stood there since 1068.

于嘉定区南翔镇的南翔寺砖塔(双塔)已有千余年历史

e Twin Pagodas in Nanxiang Town, Jiading

trict, are over 1,000 years old.

位于青浦县白鹤镇的吉云禅寺塔(青龙塔)建于821年

Black Dragon Pagoda in Baihe Town, Qingpu County, was constructed in 821.

位于徐汇区龙华镇的龙华塔相传建于242年

Longhua Pagoda in Longhua Town, Xuhui District, was originally built in 242 AD.

位于嘉定区孔庙前的古柏,树龄已有600余年

This cypress in front of the Confucian Temple in Jiading District is more than 600 years old.

位于嘉定区方泰镇的古银杏,树龄已有1200余年,是上海最古老的树木

Planted 1,200 years ago, this gingko tree in Fangtai Town, Jiading District, is the oldest surviving tree in Shanghai.

位于松江县的唐经幢建于859年,是上海地面上最古老的文物

This Stele of Buddhist Scriptures was made in 859 during the Tang Dynasty.

位于嘉定区南翔镇的古猗园始建于1746年
Guqi Garden in Nanxiang Town, Jiading
District, was built in 1746.

位于华山路的丁香花园为清末名臣李鸿章所建
Qing Dynasty Prime Minister Li Hongzhang
was the original owner of the Dingxiang
(Lilac) Garden on Huashan Road.

位于松江县的醉白池始建于1644—1661年间
Zuibai Pool in Songjiang County was built
between 1644 — 1661.

位于嘉定区的秋霞圃始建于16世纪的初期
Qiuxiapu Garden in Jiading District was constructed during the mid - 16th Century.

位于嘉定区的汇龙潭始建于1588年
Dragon Pond Garden in Jiading District dates back to 1588.

位于青浦县的曲水园始建于1745年
Qushui Garden in Qingpu County was built in 1745.

始建于1559年的豫园是上海的径曲景区
Constructed in 1559, Yuyuan Garden is a fine example of classical Chinese architecture and landscaping.

❶ 始建于247年的静安寺即将开始大规模的改扩建工程
❷ 1910年建成的徐家汇天主堂是天主教上海教区主教府所在地
❸ 位于衡山路上的国际礼拜堂
❹ 始建于1882年的玉佛寺供奉有请自缅甸的坐卧玉佛各一尊
❺ 相传始建于242年的龙华寺,是兴建中的上海龙华旅游城的主景点之一
❻ 建于1219年的嘉定孔庙设有"仰高"、"兴贤"、"育才"3座牌坊
❼ 建于1341—1368年间的松江清真寺
❽ 位于浦东新区源深路的钦赐仰殿道观

❶ With a history going back to 247 AD, the Jing'an Temple will soon undergo extensive reconstruction.

❷ This Catholic church in Xujiahui was built in 1910.

❸ The Community Church on Hengshan Road.

❹ The Jade Buddha Temple was built in 1882 to house two jade statues of Buddha from Burma.

❺ Founded in 242 AD, the Longhua Tomple is the main attraction of the Longhua Tourism Area.

❻ The Confucian Temple in Jiading District was built in 1219. It has three decorative archways.

❼ This mosque in Songjiang County was built between 1341–1368.

❽ A centuries—old Taoist temple on Yuanshen Road in Pudong.

51

"菜篮子"工程的产业化、市场化水平进一步提高
The city's "Basket Project" has created an abundant supply of vegetables.

市民外出就餐次数的增多使餐饮业频获商机
More Shanghainese like to dine out, giving a
boost to local catering business.

上海是我国商品花卉生产和销售的主要基地之一

Shanghai is a big producer and consumer of flowers.

富于投资意识和风险意识的上海人对证券市场及外汇市场的任何波动都很敏感

Many people in Shanghai are investing in stocks and are sensitive to market fluctuations.

青年消费者为商业步
行街带来强劲购买力
Young consumers are
the driving force of
local retail business.

上海人的居住条件日益改善,市区人均居住面积达9平方米

The housing condition is steadily improving in
Shanghai with per capita floor space reaching
nine square metres for urban families.

骑车上
The morning rush

郊县艺术节

A folk art festival in suburban Shanghai.

龙舟表演

A dragon boat race.

网络酒吧吸引了许多热衷"网上冲浪"的年青人
Cyber cafe has become vogue among many
young people.

自己动手做陶器，乐趣无穷
What a fun!

别具情调的小书店
A cozy bookstore

来一杯果汁，来一点好心情
Chatting over fruit juice.

久居都市的人们格外亲水，节假日
的水上乐园总是人满为患
Many of the city's water parks are
crowded like this.

各种形式的现代装置艺术颇受市民赏识
Modern art finds rich soil in Shanghai.

又一批富于冒险精神的上海人在上海中国旅行社的组织下前往新疆罗布泊荒漠探险旅游
These Shanghainese embark on an adventure tour of Lop Nur, a desert in northwest Xinjiang.

越来越多的上海人自费赴境外旅游
More and more local Chinese now travel overseas.

来自全国各地的游客在上海受到热情欢迎

Visitors from ethnic minority areas.

经济建设
ECONOMIC PROGRESS

上海是中国的老工业基地,在改革开放中,再现辉煌。1997年上海国内生产总值GDP总量超过3360亿元人民币,人均GDP逾3000美元。现在,上海已形成了6大支柱产业。1997年上海轿车产量突破了23万辆。上海钢和钢材产量居全国钢铁工业第一位。通信产业五大类产品,包括程控交换机、光纤通信、移动电话、卫星通信和终端通信等销售收入甚为可观。上海还拥有中国最大的现代化石油炼制、石油化工、合成纤维和新型塑料的联合生产企业。

上海第三产业在国民生产总值中的比重逐年提高。重点发展金融保险、商业贸易、房地产、旅游、服务、信息咨询等产业,形成了大流通、大贸易、大市场的格局。商品、金属、粮油、航运、证券等各类交易所、外汇交易中心、外国银行、保险公司、财务公司等纷纷"抢滩",上海已成为中国内外资金融机构种类、数量最多的城市之一。

上海多元化、多层次、多渠道的大外贸格局已臻雏型。目前上海与170多个国家和地区的3万多名客商建立了贸易联系。1997年口岸进出口商品总额逾587亿美元,约占全国的六分之一。

上海已成为外商投资的热土。到1997年底,上海全市累计签订利用外资合同项目20630项,其中有上百家世界著名的跨国公司投资项目近300个。世界上排名前100位的工业性跨国公司,有一半以上在上海投资。

上海农村城郊型现代化农业格局正在形成,"菜篮子工程"取得了显著成效。农村城市化步伐也大大加快。

Shanghai is one of China's old industrial bases. The reform over the past 20 years has injected the city with new vitality. In 1997, the city's GDP exceeded 336 billion yuan (US$40. 5 billion) with the per capita GDP reaching US$3,000. Steel, telecommunications, automobiles, power production equipment, petrochemicals and electric appliances have become Shanghai's six pillar industries. The city produced 230,000 cars in 1997, while its steel output is the largest in the country. China's largest petrochemical complex is also located here.

The city's service industry now represents a growing part of Shanghai's economy. Finance and insurance, commerce, real estate, tourism and information represent the key sectors for development. The city's goal is to turn Shanghai into a regional economic and trade centre. The Shanghai Stock Exchange and various specialized markets have developed rapidly in Shanghai, which also has the country's largest foreign exchange trading centre as well as many foreign banks and insurance companies.

Shanghai has developed trade relations with more than 30,000 companies in about 170 countries and regions. The value of Shanghai's imports and exports surpassed US$58.7 billion in 1977, accounting for about one－sixth of the national total.

The city has attracted more than 20,630 direct foreign investment projects, nearly 300 of which were invested by big－name multinationals. More than half of the world's top 100 industrial companies have invested in Shanghai.

Shanghai is also developing modern farming in its suburban areas. The government－supported "Basket Project" has been successful in enriching food supplies in the city.

淮海中路正通过大规模改造向国际性、现代化商业街区的目标迈进
Huaihai Road looks increasingly modern as reconstruction continues on the sides.

新老商业建筑同为
"中华商业第一街"
南京路增辉
China's No. 1 shopping
street — Nanjing Road.

空间开阔、绿地成片的徐家汇商城已成为上海商业发展最快的地区之一
Xujiahui — an upstart commercial area in southwest Shanghai.

在消费品买方市场基本形成的情况下，上海商业加速调整业态结构、商品结构和网点布局
Shanghai has changed from the sellers' market to the buyers' market. Department stores and chain stores opened one after another.

全国和世界各地的商品在上海这个大市场中集散、流通
Shanghai is a large distribution centre of domestic and foreign consumer goods.

上海的钢铁制造业通过产品结构、生产布局的调整，向精品基地方向发展
A view of the Baoshan Iron and Steel Complex.

上海口岸的集装箱吞吐量已接近300万标准箱
Shanghai Port can handle nearly 3 million TEU containers each year.

上海生产的电站成套设备销售额在全国市场连年居首位

Shanghai has been the largest supplier of power generators and related facilities for many years.

上海航天局研制的长征系列运载火箭

The Long March carrier rockets are developed and manufactured by the Shanghai Aerospace Industry Bureau.

上海汽车工业不断提高技术能级，推进产品升级换代。图为生产流水线上的豪华型桑塔纳轿车

A Santana sedan production line at the Shanghai Volkswagen Automotive Company.

上海制造的民用客机

A jet plane is being assembled at the Shanghai Aircraft Company.

上海航空公司的运能和航线辐射面逐年扩大

Shanghai Airlines' fleet and routes are expanding every year.

上海的石油化工及精细化工工业在降低物耗和能耗的同时提高了产量和质量

The Jinshan Petrochemical Complex has managed to improve efficiency by cutting the cost of energy and materials.

❶ 上海造船工业追求高科技含量和高附加值

❷ 上海电话网实现8位拨号，为信息港建设打开了空间

❸ 浦东孙桥现代农业开发区的智能型蔬菜温室

❹ 1997年，上海高新技术产业完成产值占全市工业总产值的比重为15.1%

❺ 上海生产的东海家用电脑市场占有率不断提高

❻ 上海有重点地强化应用技术的开发、中试和推广，促进产品的创新和升级

❶ High-tech, high value-added vessels are the goal of the city's shipbuilding industry.

❷ The switch to eight-digit dialing numbers marks the expansion of Shanghai's telecommunications sector.

❸ A computer-programmed greenhouse farm in Sunqiao Modern Agriculture Zone.

❹ Hi-tech manufacturing enterprises contributed 15.1% of the city's industrial output in 1997.

❺ Shanghai-made Donghai personal computers enjoy a growing market share.

❻ The city encourages the development and application of new technology to upgrade local products.

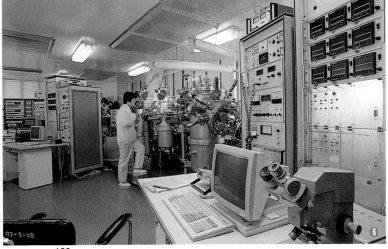

社会发展
SOCIAL LIFE

"日月光华·旦复旦兮",此语也是上海复旦大学校名的寓意,表达了追求光明、振兴教育的意义。这所世界著名大学已有90年的历史,与它同时代诞生的上海交通大学(原名南洋公学)、同济大学、圣约翰大学、沪江大学等,有的正在建设成为世界一流大学,有的虽已改名,也是生气勃勃,焕发了青春。解放后,还新建了一批现代化的新型大学。到1997年底,全市高等院校有39所,中学812所,小学1533所。此外,还有成人高校64所。上海还有一批特殊学校,如盲童学校和为外国儿童就读的国际学校等等。

海派文化是具有上海地方特征的文化。兼容并蓄、海纳百川是它的特点,上海拥有一大批文艺演出团体和著名的导演和演员。剧种有京剧、昆剧、沪剧、越剧、淮剧、音乐、舞蹈、话剧、滑稽、评弹等等。影视荧屏节目丰富多彩。上海有2个广播电台、4个电视台、4个电影制片厂和良好的拍摄基地。

上海是世界的舞台,全国以及世界著名的演员、艺术家都来这里表演。上海每两年举办一次电视节。每届电视节有世界几十个国家和地区前来参映和观摩。上海国际艺术节也是每两年举办一次,各兄弟省市和国外的著名剧团以最新最好的剧目前来参演。上海举办的国际电影节,汇集了当今世界电影文化的潮流,属于世界A级电影节。

上海还有许多具有地方特色和文化气息很浓的节日,如上海旅游节、徐汇桂花节、南汇桃花节、奉贤风筝节、闸北茶文化节、普陀花卉节等等。为上海人所喜爱的外滩、徐家汇、复兴公园等地的广场文化,也是上海的一大文化景观。

上海的福州路是著名的"文化街",一条长500米的街聚集百余家书屋报馆。现在福州路仍然保持了文化街的特色。一座现代化的上海书城正在筹建之中。到1997年底,上海有图书出版社36家,年出版图书9928种。公开发行的报纸有87种,期刊587种。

上海近年来,每年都取得2000项左右的重大科技成果。这些成果中约有三分之一达到或接近国际水平。人工合成酵母丙氨转移核糖核酸、1.56米天体测量望远镜、长征四号运载火箭、30万千瓦核电站、世界最大跨径叠合梁斜拉桥等等一大批高水平成果问世。

上海已拥有一批标志性的文化设施。如黄浦江畔的东方明珠广播电视塔,南京路上的国际广播新闻中心,人民广场中心的上海博物馆、上海大剧院,淮海中路上的上海图书馆,以及新近落成的青少年活动中心等等。上海正在建设与一流城市相适应的一流文化。

Shanghai has 39 institutions of higher learning, 812 secondary schools and 1,533 elementary schools, as well as special schools for handicapped children. The city also has a dozen schools for foreign children.

Shanghai is a big melting pot with a population largely made up of migrants. This has led to the development of the city's colourful culture. Shanghai boasts a large number of celebrated artists and performing troupes. It has two radio stations, four television stations, four film studios and several film making sites.

Many world - class musicians and artists have come to perform in Shanghai. The city regularly hosts international TV, film and art festivals. These events have drawn many domestic and overseas participants and brought an abundance of high - quality programmes to Shanghai audiences.

Other popular festivals include the Huangpu Tourism Festival, the Xuhui Osmanthus Festival, the Nanhui Peach Blossom Festival, the Fengxian Kite - flying Festival and the Zhabei Tea Festival. Outdoor concerts and performances at the Bund and other public areas have also composed unique scenes in the city's cultural life.

Fuzhou Road, known as Shanghai's "Cultural Street", has more than 100 bookstores and publishing firms. The city's 36 publishing companies released 9,928 different book titles in 1997. Meanwhile, 87 newspapers and 587 journals are published locally.

An average of about 2,000 scientific discoveries and technological breakthroughs are made in Shanghai each year, nearly one - third of which are considered to be at an advanced world level.

Shanghai boasts many landmark cultural facilities, such as the waterfront Oriental Pearl TV Tower in Pudong, Shanghai Grand Theatre and Shanghai Museum in People's Square, and the new Shanghai Library on Huaihai Road M.

上海影城
Shanghai Film Art Centre

上海广播电视国际新闻交流中心
Shanghai International Radio &
TV Exchange Centre.

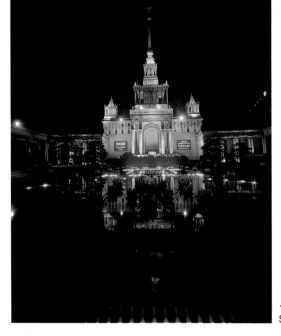

上海展览中心
Shanghai Exhibition Centre

上海音乐厅
Shanghai Concert Hall

创意新颖的城市雕塑引发人们丰富的遐想
Graceful and innovative urban sculptures in Shanghai.

全民健身运动蓬勃开展
A massive turnout of runners. The city is full of sports enthusiasts.

大学校园
Fudan University

夜自修
Campus at night

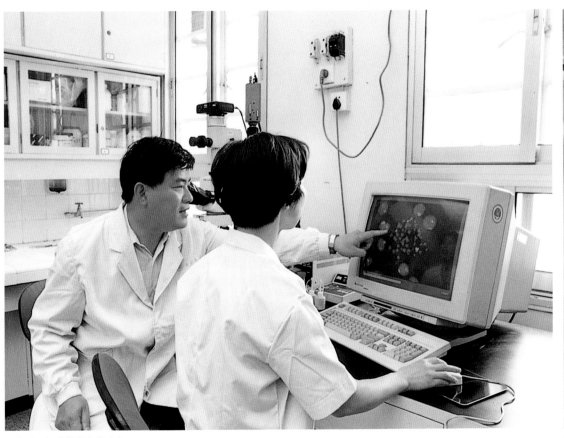

重点科研领域的学术带头人
Scientists in genetic engineering.

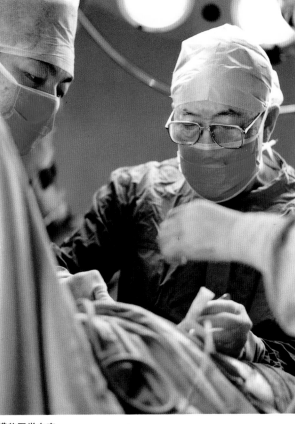

模范医学专家
Wu Mengchao, a well known Shanghai doctor.

全市学龄儿童入学率达到99.9%
The enrollment rate of school‑age children in Shanghai has reached 99.9%.

到福利院抱一抱孤儿,让他们享受到普通家庭的亲情
These people visit the Shanghai Children's Welfare Institute
to hug and talk to the orphans and let them feel family love.

癌症患者俱乐部的成员欢度"5岁"生日
These cancer patients hold "the 5th birthday" party of their club.

1997年上海常住人口出
生率为5.5‰。创建爱婴
医院、爱婴区县的工作
促进了母婴保健水平的
提高
The birth rate of permanent
Shanghai residents was 5.5
per thousand in 1997.
Most maternity hospitals
have adopted modern nursing
methods.

敬老院温暖如家
As warm as home. A scene at a local senior
citizens' home.

117

慈善募捐得到热烈响应
Charity fund raising attracts young donors.

社会服务志愿者在行动
Volunteers in action.

求职觅才上市场
A crowded job market.

下岗女工在接受电脑培训
Laid-off textile workers get training in computer applications.

① 上海国际少年儿童文化艺术节
② 上海国际电影节
③ 上海国际茶文化节
④ 上海国际电视节
⑤ 上海国际服装文化节
⑥ 上海国际魔术节
⑦ 上海国际广播音乐节
⑧ 上海国际花卉节
⑨ 上海国际艺术节

① Shanghai International Children's Art Festival
② Shanghai International Film Festival
③ Shanghai International Tea Festival
④ Shanghai International TV Festival
⑤ Shanghai International Fashion Festival
⑥ Shanghai International Festival of Magic
⑦ Shanghai International Festival of Radio Music
⑧ Shanghai International Flower Festival
⑨ Shanghai International Festival of Art

上海改革开放取得的巨大成就引起国际社会浓厚兴趣，各国政要大多将上海作为访华的必到之地

Shanghai's enormous success in reform and development has captured the world attention. Most foreign heads of state and government leaders would make a stop in Shanghai while visiting China.

美国总统比尔·克林顿及家人在上海(1998年6月)
U.S.President Bill Clinton and his Faminy visit Shanghai in June 1998.

为上海发展作出突出贡献的境外人士荣获"上海市荣誉市民"称号
Foreigners who have made outstanding contribution to the development of Shanghai are awarded the title of "Honorary Shanghai Citizen".

上海市市长国际企业家咨询会议的成员会间小憩
Participants at the International Business Leaders' Advisory Council for Shanghai Mayor take a break.

在上海工作、学习、旅游的外国人日益增多，
这座开放型的城市令他们倍感亲切

Shanghai is becoming an international city and
the number of foreigners working, studying
and travelling in Shanghai is rapidly increasing.

顾问	**ADVISER**
王仲伟	Wang Zhongwei
主编	**EDITOR IN CHIEF**
焦 扬	Jiao Yang
编委	**MEMBERS OF THE EDITING COMMITTEE**

荣牧民　王建军　李伟国　　Rong Mumin　Wang Jianjun　Li Weiguo
夏 艺　鲍克怡　　Xia Yi　Bao Keyi

责任编辑 — **CHIEF COPY EDITORS**
于鹏彬　徐福荣　　Yu Pengbin　Xu Furong

特约编辑 — **SPECIAL COPY EDITORS**
谢新发　王石泉　　Xie Xinfa　Wang Shiquan

撰文 — **WRITERS**
吴永甫　周 竞　　Wu Yongfu　Zhou Jing

装帧设计 — **GRAPHIC DESIGNERS**
赵松华　洪丽诗　　Zhao Songhua　Hong Lishi

翻译 — **TRANSLATORS**
王宁军　荣新民　　Wang Ningjun　Rong Xinmin

封面书法 — **FRONTCOVER CALLIGRAPHY**
邓 明　　Deng Ming

摄影 — **PHOTOGRAPHERS**

谢新发　达向群　欧阳鹤　纪海鹰　徐裕根　潘文龙　　Xie Xinfa　Da Xiangqun　Ouyang He　Ji Haiying　Xu Yugen　Pan Wenlong
陈志民　陈石麟　郭一江　杭凌冰　荣牧民　沈 良　　Chen Zhimin　Chen Shilin　Guo Yijiang　Hang Linbing　Rong Mumin　Shen Liang
赵中华　陈 盛　金定根　殷增善　阎维祥　吕毅民　　Zhao Zhonghua　Chen Sheng　Jin Dinggen　Yin Zengshan　Yan Weixiang　Lü Yimin
杨溥涛　张国威　丁 盛　丁志平　大田大右　王庆宏　　Yang Putao　Zhang Guowei　Ding Sheng　Ding Zhiping　Datian Dayou　Wang Qinghong
方忠麟　史兴忠　叶明训　丛名正　刘炳源　许志刚　　Fang Zhonglin　Shi Xingzhong　Ye Mingxun　Cong Mingzheng　Liu Bingyuan　Xu Zhigang
刘延平　余洪明　邹 桓　何伟铭　何香生　汪启昀　　Liu Yanping　Yu Hongmin　Zou Huan　He Weiming　He Xiangsheng　Wang Qiyun
忻正伯　陈仁群　陈光时　陈启宇　陈春轩　陈康龄　　Xin Zhengbo　Chen Renqun　Chen Guangshi　Chen Qiyu　Chen Chunxuan　Chen Kangling
邵黎阳　杨中俭　杨光亮　杨建正　金宝源　竺 钢　　Shao Liyang　Yang Zhongjian　Yang Guangliang　Yang Jianzheng　Jin Baoyuan　Zhu Gang
张 郇　张 潮　张其正　张雪雄　祖忠人　姚元祥　　Zhang Xun　Zhang Chao　Zhang Qizheng　Zhang Xuexiong　Zu Zhongren　Yao Yuanxiang
夏本建　高 原　高 峰　唐载清　崔佳德　蔡旭洲　　Xia Benjian　Gao Yuan　Gao Feng　Tang Zaiqing　Cui Jiade　Cai Xuzhou
邢 俊　姚 倬　藏志成　黄田宝　焦 扬　　Zang Zhicheng　Huang Tianbao　Jiao Yang　Xing Jun　Yao Zhuo

上海市人民政府新闻办公室编 — **COMPILED BY INFORMATION OFFICE OF SHANGHAI MUNICIPALITY**
上海辞书出版社出版 — **PUBLISHED BY SHANGHAI LEXICOGRAPHIC PUBLISHING HOUSE**

上 海　上海辞书出版社出版　上海陕西北路457号　邮政编码: 200040　上海辞书出版社发行所发行　深圳中华商务联合印刷有限公司印刷
开本787×1092　1/12　印张11　1998年6月第1版　1999年2月第2次印刷　ISBN 7-5326-0541-8/G·231　定价: 精装 98元　平装·88元
SHANGHAI Published by the SHANGHAI LEXICOGRAPHIC PUBLISHING HOUSE, 457 Shanxi Road N, Shanghai 200040 Distributed by the SHANGHAI LEXICOGRAPHIC PUBLISHING HOUSE
Printed by Shenzhen C & C Joint Printing Co., Ltd.　　First edition: June 1998 First printing, June 1998　ISBN 7-5326-0541-8/G 231　　Price: 98 yuan (hard-cover), 88 yuan (paperback)